What Other Leaders Are Saying About Todd Falcone

"Todd Falcone is one of the masters at creating connections, building rapport and closing the sale! Learn anything and everything that you can from him! It will improve your business and your life!"

- Chris Widener, author of *The Art of Influence*

"Todd Falcone uses all the tools in his toolbox to reach into your head and heart. He balances mindset and mechanics and teaches sound principles that will help you build a successful, sustainable Network Marketing business!"

- Donna Johnson, 30-year veteran of Network Marketing and multiple 7-figure earner

"Todd Falcone is a preeminent speaker, trainer and coach in the Network Marketing profession. Sales leaders that can teach with power, passion and most importantly, authenticity are rare in our profession. Todd has been a successful builder himself...very successful, and as such, he has plenty of failure stories. And...what a wonderful storyteller he is. He presents with authority, humility, power and humor. Your team will leave with powerful insights from this book."

- Richard Bliss Brooke, 40-year veteran of Network Marketing, and best selling author of *Mach II: With Your Hair on Fire, The Art of Vision & Self Motivation* and *The Four Year Career*

"This book is the no-holds-barred basic guide to building a Network Marketing business. I recommend that anyone looking for solid skills and results, with no nonsense, read this book and apply the principles now."

- Susan Sly, 7-figure earner and author of *The Have It All Woman* and *Organize Your Life*

"Todd is one of the best teachers of practical skills that are essential to building a successful Network Marketing business. The fundamentals in this book should be focused on daily until you have mastered them, and taught to your team until they have mastered them. I would get your whole team reading this book."

- Brian Carruthers, 7-figure earner and author of *Building an Empire* and *Money Mindset*

"Todd Falcone is one of the best Network Marketers I know. He is a prospecting pro and knows EXACTLY what it takes to succeed in Network Marketing."

- Jordan Adler, 7-figure earner and author of *Beach Money* and *Better than Beach Money*

"Todd Falcone is the <u>real</u> deal. He's been there and he gets it. He knows exactly what it takes to succeed, and has the unique ability to teach it. His authenticity and passion shows...and he's got the tools here to help anyone change their mindset and get to the next level in their business."

- Hayley Hobson, 7-figure earner and author of *A Beginner's Guide to Essential Oils*

FEARLESS
NETWORKING

*Create Better Connections, Invite
with Ease, Obliterate Objections,
Follow Up and Close Like a Pro!*

TODD FALCONE
THE FEARLESS NETWORKER®

CONTENTS

INTRODUCTION

The very first time I looked at Network Marketing, I was hooked! It made sense to me from the moment I was exposed to it.

What I didn't understand was exactly HOW to do the business. In fact...the first two years I did it, my results were minimal.

It wasn't until I began to really <u>study</u> what other successful people were doing and begin to <u>apply</u> those strategies that my business really took off.

I've now spent over 25 years of my life in Network Marketing and focus my full-time efforts on teaching people HOW to do this business, based on my personal experiences in the field.

Fearless Networking is really designed to be a "work" book to help people through what I've found are the biggest problem areas when it comes to prospecting and recruiting people into your business.

I designed it to literally be used <u>in the field</u> whenever you need a little helping hand in the areas of creating more powerful connections with people, inviting people to look at your business, becoming a more effective presenter, following up with greater results, enabling you to blaze through objections and helping you to close like a pro! Years ago I wrote and produced the *Little Black Book of Scripts* to be a tool for Network Marketers to use whenever they were at a loss for words when it came to prospecting. It quickly became one of the best-selling "daily use" tools in the Network Marketing profession, and still is today.

Fearless Networking is designed to help you more easily navigate through what I've found are the **six biggest problem areas in prospecting:**

1. **Rapport Building and Connecting**
2. **Inviting**
3. **Presenting**
4. **Following Up**
5. **Overcoming Objections**
6. **Closing**

Put it to use! All of the techniques and strategies taught in here have already been "field-tested" in the Network Marketing profession and proven to work.

Your Partner in Success,

Todd Falcone
The Fearless Networker®
ToddFalcone.com

CHAPTER ONE
THE FOUNDATION OF YOUR SUCCESS

My dad used to tell me, *"If you're going to do something, do it right the first time!"*

Amazing how a lesson in doing chores has served me well in business! He was referring to me doing a shoddy job of cleaning our bathroom, and made me do it all over again!

The Simple Lesson: If you're going to do something, do it right and do it as <u>best</u> you can, no matter what it is!

Your success in Network Marketing is dependent upon you building a rock solid, stable foundation of belief.

It's a <u>requirement</u> and not an option if you're seeking significance in this business.

A flimsy foundation isn't strong enough to support the weight of success, so it's imperative you build on a rock.

If you're new to me...I'll tell you right now that I'm <u>very</u> blunt. I don't beat around the bush in my trainings, soften things up or cream cheese anything. I don't have the time for it, and neither do you.

This is a "work" book, not a novel or a complete how-to book on success in Network Marketing. It's designed to be punchy, to the point, and help you in the key areas I've already mentioned.

Let Your Beliefs be Your Guide

Here's the deal. You can't succeed until you *think* it is possible for you to succeed. Until you *believe you can do it,* you have very little chance of making it here.

Operating from a position of belief is at the very foundation of your success in Network Marketing.

The areas you must establish belief in <u>right now</u> are:

1. *The Profession of Network Marketing*
2. *Your Company and Opportunity*
3. *Your Products*
4. *You*

Understand this, and let it sink in.

People do not follow or do business with individuals that lack confidence or are unclear in the direction they are heading.

Until **YOU** buy <u>your</u> story, no one is going to buy from you or do business with you.

Your beliefs in the profession, your company, your products or services and <u>you</u> are what guide you in the direction of success and accomplishment.

2

The great news is that you can work on building your beliefs right now!

Six Ways to Build Beliefs

1. ***Immerse Yourself in Success.*** Beliefs grow as you do. The more you surround yourself with positive, successful people who are supportive and encouraging, the more likely you are to grow in your beliefs of achieving success. What you read, watch and listen to makes a dramatic difference in your consciousness. Be sure to spend more time with uplifting people and less time with those that don't serve you. The best piece of advice I can give you is to become a sponge, a student of success and a student of Network Marketing. Separate yourself from negative and unsupportive people and attach yourself to those that support you and lift you up, and you'll be more likely to grow in your beliefs.

2. ***Actively Build Your Knowledge and Put it to Use.*** There's a phrase used all the time that you've probably heard. *Knowledge is power.* All by itself, knowledge is virtually useless. It's nice to have, but it's the application of the knowledge that makes the biggest difference. Be sure that you don't just learn, but immediately put into action and apply the things you learn. Once you make a new discovery, put that new "thing" you just learned into action...today. You'll grow both your business and your confidence all at the same time. Don't allow a new piece of knowledge to sit idle and unused. Put it to use today!

3

3. ***Create and Collect Stories.*** Beliefs grow when they're evidenced by results. When you see an individual get results on your product or in your business, it builds on your belief. As <u>you</u> create results, either with your products or your business, your beliefs take dramatic leaps forward. Take action, work on building your business and <u>create</u> your story. If you want to know if it works, then work until you see the result and <u>know</u> that it works.

4. ***Take Action Daily.*** Your consistent <u>daily</u> actions and efforts in building your business directly contribute to growing your personal confidence. You can't get good at something you don't do. Daily action, in spite of not knowing everything, helps you to learn, earn and grow in your beliefs. Remember this. You don't need to know <u>everything</u> in order to get started. A lot of your learning will take place *because* of the actions you take, and your beliefs will grow as a result of those actions.

5. ***Practice.*** This is something I can't say enough about. Professionals are professionals <u>because</u> they practice. If you want to get good at this business and feel confident doing it, then you need to spend regular time in practice. Take time to practice your approaches, your invites, and your presentations. Anything you do in this business to make money should be practiced ahead of time. Build practice into your regular routine and you'll find yourself quickly improving your skills and your confidence at the same time.

6. *__Regularly Attend Events.__* The more plugged-in you are, the better off you'll be. Events serve many purposes, including helping you to not only learn, but be in an environment that fosters belief. The more events you attend, the more likely you are to grow both your business and your beliefs.

Once you are operating from a state of belief about this business model, your company and your abilities to do it, you literally become unstoppable. No one can touch you!

They can try...but a person operating on a solid foundation of belief cannot be toppled, shaken or waivered. That's the power of belief.

A lot of people want to focus simply on the skill development side, but what you will find is that success is far more mindset than most people expect.

In fact...I've heard Tony Robbins say that success is 80% psychology and 20% mechanics.

Clearly...you need both to succeed.

Focusing time on developing your success "consciousness" is going to help you get better results when it comes to the mechanics, the "how to" part of this business.

If you'd like to focus on building up your mental toughness, you can download a free copy of *__7 Steps to Mental Toughness__* from my training site here: toddfalcone.com/free-gift-4.

CHAPTER TWO
UNDERSTANDING WHY PEOPLE BUY

People buy for many reasons, but the <u>one thing</u> you really need to be aware of is this: *People buy from those they like and trust.*

If you want to build your business faster and move more of your products or services, then you've got to work on making sure that people like you and trust you.

What Makes People Like You?

To put it simply, when you make another person *feel good*, you're moving in the right direction!

There's a phrase that comes directly from the book *How to Win Friends and Influence People,* and that phrase is:

"Be genuinely interested, not interesting."

The more interest you show in another person, and the more <u>genuine</u> it is, the more they're going to like you and feel good about you.

7

Instead of being the person who always talks, brags and has to be the star of the show, turn your attention to them and who they are, and they'll end up falling all over you.

Ask questions. Be interested. Listen! It's not hard. People love it when you show interest in them!

What Makes People Trust You?

I'll tell you this now. You want to work on your ability to influence others. If you didn't know that, now you do.

Leadership is influence.

Influence is defined as *the ability to change attitudes, beliefs, opinions or behaviors to a pre-determined outcome.*

Effective leadership is rooted in trust.

The way you build your business, make more sales and grow is to consistently act in such a way where people trust you.

Clearly, trust is built by telling the truth!

There's never a need to exaggerate, go overboard, fib, or tell a lie. The truth is always good enough. If you don't tell the truth, it will come back to bite you, and HARD! It's simply not worth it.

How exactly is trust built? Trust is built through consistency over time.

If you want more people to trust you, to believe in you, to follow you, or buy from you...then what they need to see from you is consistency.

I don't necessarily mean that they need to see you be consistent in your business, although that's important. I mean be consistent in your behaviors and actions.

Ask yourself a few questions and see how you stand on the subjects of reliability and follow-through:

1. *Reliability.* Am I seen as being reliable? Do people see me as someone that can always be counted on?

2. *Follow-Through:* Do I consistently stick to my commitments or am I constantly changing my mind? Do people know me as someone who always finishes what they started?

Building Your Emotional Bank Accounts

Look at your relationships this way. They are like banks. Just like you can't make a withdrawal from an empty bank account, you can't make a withdrawal from a relationship where you've made no emotional deposits.

If the only time you call or contact someone is when you want something from them, you're not going to get it. And...in a business like Network Marketing that is driven by people, you want to do everything you can to build and maintain strong, trusting relationships with them.

Make sure that you are making regular deposits into the "emotional bank accounts" of the people you know.

Here are a few easy examples:

- Make a call and catch up with someone you haven't talked to in a long time. <u>Be the initiator.</u> Reach out and say "hello", and do so with no hidden agenda.

- Send a text message to a friend and say something nice like, *"Hope your day is going great! Was just thinking about you and wanted to say how much I appreciate having you in my life!"*

- Send a random card or small gift when they <u>least</u> expect it! This one blows people's minds, especially when it's not on their birthday or anniversary! You don't need to spend a bunch of money, but a random gift out of the blue is mind boggling to people. Most people love surprises!

- Invite them out to lunch or coffee. This isn't to pitch them your business, but to simply <u>grow</u> the relationship.

- Send them something on a subject they love! If your friend loves a particular band, and you see that they are coming to town...send them a text that says, *"Hey...did you see that Pink Floyd is coming to town?"* You could forward them an article, a blog post you read, anything that <u>they</u> might find interesting...and it shows them that you care, and you're thinking of them.

- Reach out to someone on FaceBook you haven't connected with in a while and spark up a conversation.

There are a lot of very simple steps you can take to maintain and improve the quality of the relationships you have with people you know.

The more you stay connected with people, the better off your business will be. Your contacts are a lot more likely to be open to looking at your business or sampling your product if they see you as someone who has made an effort to stay in regular contact with them.

CHAPTER THREE
BREAK THE ICE AND BUILD RAPPORT

We've already determined that people prefer to buy from and do business with individuals they feel good about.

Not too many people get excited about doing business with someone they don't like very much! Let me ask you, *"Do you get excited about giving money to someone you don't like?"* I didn't think so!

Your friends already like you and know you...it's why we call them friends. There's typically no ice breaking or rapport building that's necessary when it comes to having a conversation with people we already know well, because we are already in a state of rapport with them.

What is Rapport?

Rapport is the presence of alignment with one or more individuals.

It's the ability to relate to others in a way that creates trust and understanding. It's affinity, a feeling of a bond, or connection with someone.

When you're <u>in rapport</u> with someone, things feel easy and effortless. There's a connection, or a feeling of being "on the same page." You can relate to one another, and there's no tension present.

Knowing that definition now, you can easily see why it's so important to be IN rapport with people if you're looking to grow your business.

It's pretty critical to be comfortable in sparking up a conversation with someone you don't yet know and be able to break the ice with those people.

How to Break the Ice with People

The term "breaking the ice" is a very old one that is commonly used to describe removing the tension or awkwardness in the beginning of a conversation or relationship.

It typically precedes the rapport building process. It can also be referred to as a conversation starter.

Whenever we meet a new person or begin a conversation... it's important to do things that remove the tension (the ice) from the conversation, and *warm* things up a bit.

It's natural to be a little nervous, especially when approaching someone new. We don't know what they're like or how they'll respond. It's an unknown. Are they mean and grumpy? Or, are they as sweet as apple pie?

There are lots of ways to break the ice with people. For the sake of this book, I'm going to keep it really simple for you to get better at starting or warming up your conversations.

A couple things to keep in mind that will serve you well not only in breaking the ice, but also advancing the level of rapport you have with someone is making direct eye contact and having a smile on your face.

Remember...you're looking to connect with someone.

Direct eye contact is critical! Everyone's heard the phrase that the *"eyes are the windows to the soul"*. People are not likely to trust someone who is unable to make direct eye contact with them.

In fact...people whose eyes constantly dart around, looking everywhere but the person they're talking to, are more often considered shady or not trustworthy. It's as if they're hiding something. Eye contact is a must if you're seeking to create a real connection with someone.

And...as much as I shouldn't have to say this, put a smile on your face! Even if you have to consciously summon it up, that is something you want to work on.

Try this one on for size. Walk into a room with a big frown on your face and see how well you're received.

Then, walk in someplace else with a big, beaming smile on, and see what happens. I promise you this, you will see and feel a noticeable difference in how you are received by the people you make eye contact with in that room.

Smiles are door openers and make people *feel* good. They <u>literally</u> release endorphins in your body, which trigger a positive feeling. People are drawn to positivity. When they view you as someone who is happy, positive and a pleasure to be around...they'll want to spend time with you.

Four Ways to Break the Ice and Start a Conversation

1. **The Basic Greeting with a Smile.** *"Hey There! How you doing?"* Simply greeting someone with a little eye contact and a smile is often enough to get a conversation going.

2. **Give a Genuine Compliment.** *"Wow! Those boots are awesome! Where'd you find those?"* Actively be looking for things that you can compliment people on.

3. **Ask a Question.** *"Is this place always this busy?"* Or, *"Do you know where I can find a really good coffee shop in town?"* Questions get answers. And, answers are the beginning of a conversation if you've taken the time to ask.

4. **Comment on the Obvious.** If you see something in their office where you're meeting them, like a picture of them holding up a trophy fish they caught, say something like, *"Wow...what kind of fish is that? That thing is HUGE!"* Look for things to comment on that are obvious and use them as conversation starters to break the ice.

Understanding How the Three Foot Rule Really Works

In Network Marketing you've likely heard about the Three Foot Rule. It essentially means sparking up a conversation and talking to people that are in close proximity and talking to them about your business.

Here's the thing. I <u>never</u> walk up to stranger and say, *"Hey! Do you want to hear about how to make some money?"*

In fact...that's <u>not at all</u> how the Three Foot Rule works. People will look at you cross-eyed or run in the opposite direction if you do that.

Again, the Three Foot Rule does <u>not</u> mean that you jump all over someone and immediately start telling them about your products or business.

It <u>does</u> mean that it's a really great idea that if someone is near you and you're looking to grow your business that it's an opportunity for you to make a connection that <u>can</u> lead to a conversation about your business.

Proximity is important. If I find myself in a situation where someone is reasonably close to me and I can come up with a <u>reason</u> to start a conversation and say something, I will.

People ask me all the time, *"Todd, what do you say?"*

My answer is, *"I don't know. Something. I say whatever comes to mind with whatever situation I find myself in. And, it depends on the situation."*

As Network Marketers, we are always looking for new customers and new people to put into our business... and life dishes out all sorts of opportunities to meet new people, as long as we <u>open ourselves</u> to the possibilities of making new introductions.

The key in opening yourself up to meeting new people is keeping your eyes open, figuratively speaking.

No one literally walks around with their eyes closed. But oftentimes the way they operate is "as-if" their eyes are closed.

The more times you can meet the eyes of another human being, the more likely it is you'll end up having a conversation with them.

And again...it can start with something as simple as eye contact, a smile and saying something like I've mentioned before:

A Simple Greeting: *"Hey...how's your day going?"*

The Obvious: *"What an incredible day today!"* Yes, you can talk about the weather!

A Genuine Compliment: *"That's a beautiful dress!"*

A Question: *"What kind of dog is that?"*

You get the picture! Say <u>something.</u> Stop letting opportunities pass you by! You'll figure it out. It's just a conversation. We have them every day!

Removing the Pressure for Better Performance

Let me give you a very powerful piece of advice that will help you remove the nervousness in meeting and greeting new people for your business.

Forget about your business for a moment.

Yes...you have a business. And yes, I'm sure you'd love to recruit this new person in front of you.

The best thing you can do is to *remove the pressure* from having to perform or somehow move the conversation to your product or business.

If you can simply move your mindset into simply meeting this new person, saying hello and starting a "regular old non-business conversation", which we do all the time, nearly every day of our lives...you'll be able to easily summon the courage to say something to a stranger.

Why? Simple. You don't have this overwhelming pressure in your head about how you're going to somehow transition into a conversation about your business. You can allow it to happen a little more naturally.

So many people end up saying NOTHING to a person because they're so worried about what to say to them because their focus is all placed on the idea of *"How can I share my business with this person?"*

Once you remove that pressure, it's <u>just</u> a conversation. We have them all the time and never think twice about it.

It's the <u>business</u> that creates the pressure and the fear in most cases.

Temporarily removing it from the occasion can be *just enough* for most people to act instead of passing by yet another great opportunity to make another connection.

Building and Maintaining Rapport

As I mentioned earlier, rapport is a sense of alignment with another person or group of individuals.

Remember again that people buy from those they like and trust.

The more we are like them or *similar* to them, the more likely they will like us and ultimately want to do business with us.

Yes. That's a lot of likes, but you get the point!

In rapport building, you are seeking to be more like or similar to the person you are speaking with, whether in person or on the telephone.

Mirroring Their Behavior

There are several very easy ways to establish and maintain a state of rapport with people.

Mirroring: Mirroring is exactly what it sounds like. It is simply mimicking the subtle behaviors with whomever we are communicating.

Much like when you wave at yourself in the mirror, you see a "mirror reflection" of you waving back. That's what we do in developing rapport.

When we mirror a person's behavior, we become more like them, and in turn, because we are perceived as similar to them, they're more likely to like us. The key word is subtlety. You don't want to be seen as obviously mimicking someone's behavior or being perceived as a "copycat".

Mirroring can be accomplished by copying any of the following:

- *The tempo, pitch, tone or volume of their language.*
- *Their body language or gestures.*
- *Specific vocabulary or types of words they use.*

If someone speaks fast, you speak fast.
If they speak slowly, you speak slowly.
If they speak loud, you speak loud.
If someone leans forward, you lean forward.
If someone crosses their legs, you cross your legs.

Again...be careful and make absolutely sure that what you are doing isn't obvious. Remember...subtlety is crucial.

If someone uses specific types of words or language, do your best to talk *like* them.

I don't want to go too far down the rabbit hole on this subject. The key point is mirroring how they communicate.

I'm typically fairly loud and fast in my natural way of speaking. However, if you've ever heard me speak to a prospect on the phone and they are very soft spoken, you will notice that I immediately mirror their softness in how they talk. You may have to consciously think about this at first. But, as you put this into practice regularly...it will eventually become automatic for you and you won't even have to think about it.

Finding Mutual Commonalities or Connections

Isn't it interesting how quickly we connect with someone we have something in common with, and how *instant* that connection occurs?

You meet someone who loves a particular band, sports team, or is from the same city you lived in, the connection is instantaneous.

As you are getting to know someone and finding out more about them, it's easy to discover things you may have in common.

Ask questions like:

"Where are you from?"
"What part of the country are you in?"
"What do you do for a living?"
"Do you have kids?"
"What do you do for fun?"

All of those questions can lead to you being able to deepen the level of rapport you have with a person.

Think for a second. When was the last time you met someone who you had something in common with and how <u>easy</u> it was to talk to that individual?

I met a guy at the gym a while back who was wearing a Seattle Seahawks t-shirt. I'm from Seattle and a big Seahawks fan.

I walked up and said, *"Go Hawks!"*

We immediately began a conversation about the team, which led to me asking him where he was from, and come to find out...he grew up right around the corner from me! That conversation was <u>effortless</u>, and the rapport was immediate.

Find ways to ask questions and discover things you don't yet know, which will lead you into creating a deeper level of rapport with people you meet.

The more questions you ask, the more likely you are to discover things you have in common with them.

CHAPTER FOUR
SIMPLE AND EFFECTIVE INVITES

What's an invite? It's exactly what it sounds like. It's a simple and friendly request to do something.

When it comes to Network Marketing, one of the key skills you need to master is the invite.

Again...for the sake of this training, I'm going to keep the scripting simple.

I have an entire book dedicated to scripts and invites, called *Little Black Book of Scripts*, which can be found at littleblackbookofscripts.com.

Simple Warm Market Invites

The "I Found Something" Invite

"Hey _____ it's _____ . How's it going? I just found something that I'm really excited about and I think it's going to be BIG! I'd love to show it to you. When would you have (the amount of time you need) for me to show you what I'm up to?"

Important Note: If they ask what it is...and many of them will, simply tell them that it's exactly why you want to meet with them. No need to be evasive. Just book the appointment.

The "I've Launched a New Business" Invite

"Hey _____ it's _____. How's it going? I've just launched a new business and I'm looking for some people to help me with it. I'd love to get together with you and show you what I'm up to. When would you have (the amount of time you need) for me to run it by you?"

Important Note: Be sure not to say things like *"I'm thinking about starting a business"* or *"I'm looking into starting a business"* because it shows a lack of commitment on your part. People follow decisive individuals.

The "Feedback" Invite

"Hey _____ it's _____. How's it going? Listen...I just got involved in a new business and am looking to get some feedback on it. Would you be willing to meet with me and take a look at what I'm doing?"

I could give you loads and loads of different openings for warm market invites. However, there's no need to complicate things here.

Keep it simple. All you're doing is inviting someone to take a look at what you're up to.

Remember...don't explain anything on the telephone and attempt to present your business without using whatever tools you have within your company that are designed to do that for you.

Simply do the invite and set the appointment. Then... when you meet with them, either now on the phone or in person at a future time, you can lay it all out for them.

Use your tools! Most Network Marketing companies have tools that do a great job of presenting _for_ you. Make sure you take advantage of using them, because that's exactly what they are designed to do!

My All-Time Favorite Question to Ask

When it comes to asking a specific pique interest question, I'm sure you can find some room to utilize this one in your day-to-day marketing efforts.

"Do you at all keep your options open in terms of making money outside of what you are currently doing?"

It's simple and to the point. And...I've made more money asking that question to people than I can even begin to calculate.

If they say YES, and many people do, simply set an appointment or schedule a time where you can show them what you are up to and how they can benefit from working with you.

By the way, this question works very well with people you are just getting to know.

If you've taken the time to say hello, break the ice, and establish a little rapport, you can easily segue into asking this question as an example:

"Let me ask you something. Do you at all keep your options open in terms of making money outside of what you are doing in your real estate business?"

Once you have someone that has agreed to meet with you or attend a presentation, the next step is doing the presenting.

More than likely, you will be doing some recruiting in both the warm and cold market. For those of you who venture off into doing cold market recruiting, I have a little **Cheat Sheet** that can help you. You can get it directly off of my site and download it for free anytime: ToddFalcone.com/free-gift-2.

Applying SPIN Selling to Network Marketing

I read a book several years ago on the subject of selling called *SPIN Selling* by Neil Rackham. His book was based on the studies of 35,000 sales calls used by top sales forces from around the world.

In that book, he talks about four different types of questions:

1. **S**ituation Questions
2. **P**roblem Questions
3. **I**mplication Questions
4. **N**eed-Payoff Questions

That's where the term SPIN is derived. In this section, I want to show you how I've adapted the use of those types of questions in Network Marketing, so you can be even more prepared in your prospecting calls for your business.

The quality of your questions make a significant impact on the results you get with people. In fact...I'd go as far as to say that they are determining factors on whether or not a sale is made.

While I don't consider putting someone into my business as making a sale...there is power and application in the use of these types of questions in our profession.

In making sales of your products or services that your company markets, you may find these types of questions even more useful.

Situation Questions

This type of question deals with the facts about your prospect's current situation.

Here are some Situation Question examples:

"Tell me more about your job?"

"How many hours a week do you work?"

"Are they paying you enough where you can save money for retirement?"

Problem Questions

Problem Questions uncover a prospect's pain or dissatisfaction and focus on that pain or dissatisfaction while helping to clarify exactly what that problem is.

Here are a few examples of Problem Questions:

"Are you excited to get up and go to work every day?"

"Is it at all frustrating for you that you work so many hours?"

"How easy is it for you to put away money every month?"

Implication Questions

These types of questions discuss the effects of the problem, before talking about solutions...and help to develop the serious nature of the problem to increase your prospect's motivation to change.

Here are a few examples of Implication Questions:

"Do you think you'll ever be in a place again where going to work is exciting for you and you look forward to it?"

"Has working so many hours affected your family life at all?"

"What happens when you retire and haven't saved any money?"

Need-Payoff Questions

These get your prospect to tell you about their wants and needs and the benefits that your opportunity or products offer, rather than you having to explain them.

Here are a few Need-Payoff Questions:

"How would you feel if you got up every morning and were excited to start working?"

"How would you feel if you had complete time freedom and could work when and where you wanted, without ever having to report to anyone?"

"If you could make an extra thousand dollars a month, how would that help you in saving for retirement?"

Let me put it all together for you in this simple example so you can see how these questions might work for you in a prospecting situation.

YOU: (Situation Question) *"Tell me more about your job."*

YOUR PROSPECT: *"Well...I've been working there for about 15 years. It's pretty good, but I've hit the top of my pay scale."*

YOU: (Situation Question) *"How many hours a week are you working right now?"*

YOUR PROSPECT: *"Most weeks I put in about 50 hours... and I commute an hour in each direction."*

YOU: (Problem Question) *"Does working so many hours and being gone so long ever get frustrating to you?"*
YOUR PROSPECT: *"It's frustrating all the time, to be honest with you."*

YOU: (Problem Question) *"I bet...that's a lot of time away from home. Has working so many hours affected your family life at all?"*

YOUR PROSPECT: *"My wife hates the fact that I'm gone so much. And I hate the fact that I only see my kids for a few minutes every night before they go to bed."*

YOU: *"Ouch. How would you feel if you had complete time freedom and could work when and where you wanted, and could spend a lot more time at home with your family?"*

YOUR PROSPECT: *"Are you kidding? If I could be home with my family more and not have to work so hard, I'd be the happiest man alive!"*

YOU: *"If I could show you a plan to help you get your time back, make the same kind of money you're making...if not more, and be able to see your wife and kids more often, is that something you'd like to see?"*

YOUR PROSPECT: *"Of course. What is it?"*

At that point in the conversation, you'd obviously schedule a time to present your opportunity to this person.

When I started writing this book, I wasn't going to include this section, because it's a little more detailed and in depth.

However, for those of you reading this who want to have every advantage possible, I wanted to share that with you.

CHAPTER FIVE
GIVING BETTER PRESENTATIONS

Every Network Marketing company has their way of presenting the business or products to someone.

It may be an online video, a webinar, a flip chart, an in-home presentation, a weekly meeting, a recorded call, a CD, a DVD, or something else.

The KEY for you is to find out exactly WHAT presentation people are using within your company and use the tool or tools that are available to you.

Ask the people in your upline leadership team, *"What is the best tool or tools to present this business to someone?"*

"What have you found to be the most effective way of presenting our business to a new prospect?"

This book isn't going to tell you HOW or WHAT you should use in presenting your products or business. Get with your leadership team and find out what's working right now...and use it.

The great thing is that in almost every case, you have resources available to you that do an incredible job of presenting the business for you, so you don't actually have to be doing the presentation yourself.

The secret to giving better presentations is to use tools to do most of the work for you!

Even though you are, more than likely, going to use some type of presentation tool to do most of the work for you, I would highly advise you to educate yourself to the point of being able to present your business, with or without the use of a tool.

In other words, most professional Network Marketers could very easily explain to a person exactly who their company is, what their product is about, and why a person should consider partnering with them.

Becoming a Better Presenter

As I've already mentioned, when it comes to presenting, use your tools! It's what they are designed to do!

However, you do want to become a better presenter so that you can become as effective as possible in every situation.

Here are my suggestions on becoming a better presenter:

1. **Know Your Company, Their History, Your Products and Your Compensation Plan.** The more personal knowledge you have about your company and what you market, the better you'll be at talking to people about them. Set some time aside to work on being the most knowledgeable person you can be about the company you are in, and what you are marketing.

2. **Pay Close Attention to Your Tools.** Another really great way of improving your personal presentation skills is to pay very close attention to what they say and how they say it. For example, if I used a 20-minute online video as my presentation tool...I would make it my point to virtually memorize every point that is made during that presentation. You don't have to know it by heart, but the more you study it...the better you're going to be if you need to say something to someone.

3. **Volunteer to Participate.** Anytime you can step-up and volunteer to help in your business, it creates a new opportunity for your presentation skills to grow. Volunteer to help host a training call, take introductions on a webinar, share your testimonial, or even be a part of a live presentation. They're all fantastic opportunities to develop your skills.

4. **Practice Your Presentation.** You'll hear me say this more than once in this book. The more practicing you do, the better you're going to be. Practice leads to improvement. I speak for a living...and yet I <u>always</u> practice my presentation before giving it. Even if it's a presentation I've done a hundred times before...I still practice it.

Becoming a better presenter takes work. If you have the willingness and the desire to get better...and take action on a regular basis to help you grow those skills, you <u>will</u> become better at presenting your products or business, with or without the use of a sales tool.

Once they've watched, listened to or reviewed your presentation, it's time to "take their temperature."

Taking Their Temperature

Let's move the ball forward a bit. You set the appointment, met with your prospect and presented your business to them.

The first thing I like to do is <u>take their temperature</u> to see how hot or cold they are based on what they just looked at or heard.

I do this in one of two ways.

Ask Them What They Liked the Most

I prefer to ask someone how they *felt* about what they just reviewed rather than asking them what they think, and I do so by asking the following question:

"<u>What did you like the most about what you just saw?</u>"

That question forces the prospect to respond with something they liked the most. The question is designed to elicit a specific and <u>positive</u> response. Let them tell you what they liked the most. It will give you a very good idea of their interest level.

Ask Them to Rate Themselves

Another really great way of taking their temperature and seeing how hot or cold they are is to ask them:

"That gives you a really good idea of who we are and what we do. Let me ask you, if you were going to rate yourself on a scale of 1 to 10, one being 'not at all interested' and 10 being 'I'm ready to get started right now', how would you rate yourself?"

When you ask the 1 to 10 question, people will literally tell you how hot or cold they are, and it gives you the opportunity to find out what it would take to get them to a 10. When they give you a number below a 10, ask them:

"What would you need to consider yourself a 10?"

It's a simple and natural question to ask.

There's no coercion or manipulation here. All you're doing is finding out what's missing for them in order to shift their interest level from simply getting involved to fully engaging in the business with you.

Based on their response, you'll be able to either enroll them right then and there, or provide them whatever additional information they need to make a relaxed and informed decision.

By the way, this is an ideal time to bring in an upline expert or your sponsor on a 3-way call to help answer any remaining questions they might have, as well as provide some additional social validation.

CHAPTER SIX
GAINING CONTROL OF YOUR FOLLOW UP

In almost every case, you will need to follow up with your prospect.

Very seldom do people join after the first point of contact or presentation. Yes, some people will join immediately after having reviewed your initial presentation. But, many of them will need additional information so they can make what they feel is a relaxed and totally informed decision.

You may have heard the phrase: *The Fortune is in the Follow up.*

It's true. Most of your money will be made in this business by having the willingness and the patience to follow up with people who have looked at your products or business presentation.

Based on how they respond, you may need to get additional information to that person and schedule a follow up call or meeting to address any further questions they might have.

Let me give you some very direct, straight talk!
People you meet with and present your business to
expect you to get back to them!

Don't be a ball-dropper and fall short on your follow
through. Finish what you started! They're expecting you
to get back to them.

If you SAY you're going to do something, do it! Too often,
I see people in this business that initiate, but don't finish.

The business comes to those who <u>finish</u> what they started.

Find Out What They Need and Give it to Them

After I've taken someone's temperature and find that
they are interested, but need more information I'll
ask them, *"What specifically do you want more
information about?"*

Let them <u>tell you</u> what they need to be able to make a
comfortable decision for themselves.

Typically, people will want more information in one of the
following areas:

- More detailed information about the company, its
  background and history.
- A desire to try the products first.
- A deeper understanding of how the compensation
  plan works and how they are paid.

- To know more about how to actually make money and the activities they'd be involved in if they decided to join.

Once you find out what's missing, provide them the information and schedule a time to get back to them.

Critical Point: Don't ever assume that they have the ability to watch or review something you're about to send them. For example, I would never simply send someone an audio CD without first asking them if they have a CD player. Most people own them, but don't assume it. You don't want to ship out a CD to someone and find out that they don't even own a CD player!

How soon do you follow up? As soon as possible!

There's no 48-hour rule or "wait a week" rule for getting back to someone.

Ideally, you want to get back to the person the moment they've reviewed whatever further information it is that you've provided them.

Here's an example of what I'd say in setting up my follow up call or meeting:

"I'll email you over a video on the compensation plan and a bit more history on the company. It should take you about 45-minutes to get through that. When in the next 24 hours will you have 45-minutes to go through that?"

Notice that I didn't simply say, *"When will you get around to it?"*

I asked them, *"When in the next 24 hours..."*

It shows a sense of urgency and also shows that you are serious and committed in your business.

If I'm talking to my prospect on Tuesday at 4 p.m., and they respond with, *"I can't get to it until Thursday night when I get home from work",* my response will likely be:

"Great. I can either call you back at 6:30 p.m. or 8 p.m. on Thursday night. Which one works better for you?"

When scheduling a follow up call or meeting, always give them an either-or option.

It's far more powerful than asking, *"When can I call you back?"*

If neither works, schedule a time that does work.

Let's say for the sake of this example that my prospect says, *"I can meet with you at 6:30 p.m. Thursday."* Here's how I would firm up the meeting:

"Great. I'll be calling you on Thursday at 6:30 p.m. to answer any questions you have. Can you do me a favor? Write down my phone number. 555-1212. If something comes up and, for whatever reason, you didn't have a chance to get through the information, just give me a call, and I'll be happy to reschedule you."

Again, you're showing that you are busy and serious about your business. People like doing business with those that are committed and focused.

Now...of course, when 6:30 p.m. rolls around, make sure that you call them! Don't call 15-minutes early, don't be late, and certainly don't forget about the appointment you set. Put it in your calendar and stick to it!

What Happens During a Follow Up

The purpose of the follow up call or meeting is to address your prospect's questions and enroll them into your business, get them using your products or services, or lastly...ask for a referral if they choose neither.

The format of the call or meeting is pretty simple.

"This is Todd Falcone. Did you have a chance to get through the information I sent you?"

If YES, then I'll immediately follow up with:

"Great! Do you have any questions?"

I welcome questions from my prospects and am happy to answer them.

Simply do your best to answer their questions...and if you're new or don't know the answers, this is another great opportunity to do a 3-way call with someone in your upline leadership team who has more experience than you do.

The follow up call or meeting is an opportunity for you to further feel out where they stand, address their questions or concerns, and help move them closer to a decision.

What Happens if They "No Show" on Your Follow Up

The reality is that no matter how good you are or how great your company is, people often don't stick to their commitments.

Your job is to be professional and be the best person you can be. If they choose to be flaky, that's their choice. Don't allow it to bother you. The best Network Marketers on the planet have people "no show" on follow up appointments. It's simply part of the business.

Here's what I typically do with people who flake out on follow up appointments.

If I call them and they don't answer, I'll leave a message with something like,

"Hey there. This is Todd Falcone getting back to you for our 6:30 p.m. appointment. Obviously, something must have come up for you. Not a problem. I've got back-to-back appointments over the next couple of hours so you may not be able to reach me live. Give me a call back when you are free and we can re-schedule at a time that's convenient for both of us. I know you have my number, but here it is again. 555-1212. Chat with you soon."

Don't sound desperate. Don't sound angry. Simply be professional. Show them that you are busy and that they're not the only person you're working with, and leave a message.

If they call you back, that's a great sign that they are interested. If they don't get back to you, then call them back.

However, I typically wait 24 to 48 hours before calling them back a second time.

After I've waited 24 to 48 hours and haven't heard back from them, I'll leave this type of message:

"Hey there. This is Todd Falcone checking in. We had a meeting scheduled a couple days ago. If you're still serious about talking a bit further about this business, give me a call. Here's my number. 555-1212. I'm happy to chat with you whenever you are free."

After I've left the second message and NOT received a call back from them, I'll wait few days and leave them one more message that may be something like this:

"Hey There. This is Todd Falcone getting back to you one more time. I haven't heard back from you, so I'm assuming you're either really busy or changed your mind about this business. No worries. If you decide you want to talk further, give me a call and we can catch up then. Take care!"

The last thing you want to do is sound desperate or angry with the person. You've done your job of being professional and on your follow up game. If they choose to be flaky, then let them be that way and move on.

If you want to give yourself an easy rule for follow up, I'd suggest the "Three Strikes and You're Out" rule, which means following up with them three times (if they haven't responded back to you), and then moving on.

You can always get back to them at a later time.
If I've followed up with a prospect three times and they haven't called me back, I'll put them on my back burner and get back to them in a month or two.

Timing is everything for people. You may end up calling them a month down the road and come to find out that they simply had a lot going on in their life and didn't have the time to make starting a business a priority.

CHAPTER SEVEN
OVERCOMING COMMON OBJECTIONS

There are a number of common objections or questions we get in Network Marketing, and it's important you learn how to address concerns and help to overcome any objections.

Don't be afraid of objections. To me, receiving an objection from someone shows me that they have interest, but they're concerned about something and simply need a little help in having their concern addressed.

How Professionals Treat Objections

There are some important things to keep in mind when it comes to being a professional in handling common objections and tough questions from your prospects.

1. Don't ever take it personally. If someone says NO to you or responds with a specific objection, they are not rejecting you!

This is one of the most important things you need to understand about this business. I get it. No one likes being rejected. Human beings love being accepted. It's how we are. This is BUSINESS.

I hear people in Network Marketing talk about "being rejected." That's really <u>not</u> the case! What those people are <u>choosing</u> to do is take it personally. And...it is a CHOICE!

If someone says NO or has an objection or tough question, it isn't you. Trust me when I say that. They're really saying NO to themselves. They aren't rejecting you personally. I cannot express to you enough how important it is for you to get this.

I get people who say NO or have objections <u>all the time!</u>

Professionals make the conscious decision to not allow someone else's behavior to alter how they feel. It's simply part of the business!

2. Don't get defensive or argue with a prospect. I realize that we are all passionate and excited about our businesses and want people to see it like we do, but the last thing you want to do is get into an argument or appear defensive with someone.

You'll be a lot better off being calm, cool and collected when people respond to you with tough questions or objections.

3. Allow your confidence to be your guide. I mentioned this very early on in the book, and it will serve you well when it comes to overcoming objections.

Your knowledge that the profession of Network Marketing is a $180 billion dollar global industry with over 100 million people involved worldwide should be enough to soothe your nerves.

When you operate from a state of conviction and assuredness, showing your excitement and passion in all that you do, you're going to be much better suited for addressing these common questions than if you're always worried about someone asking you a tough question.

How you choose to respond to people will make a big difference in the outcome. Remember, objections are actually GOOD. It means they're interested!

4. Seek out help when you need it! On your way to becoming a true professional and expert in addressing questions and objections, you may need to reach out for assistance.

Even though I'll be covering HOW to respond to people in the next section, don't be afraid to reach out to an upline or expert in your company if you get an objection and don't quite know how to handle it.

In fact...any time you get a tough question or objection that you feel you didn't handle so well, write it down. Then, go ask someone who has a lot more experience than you do and find out how *they* would handle that specific objection. That way, in the future, you'll be better suited and prepared when that question comes along.

When it comes to addressing questions and dealing with objections, it's important to keep in mind that your prospect wants to be comfortable and ultimately feel good about the following questions before proceeding:

"Does it work?"
"Is it real?"
"Can I do it?"
"Will it work for me?"
"Will you help me?"

Be sure to keep that in mind as you go about your prospecting efforts and are met with objections along the way.

The Feel, Felt, Found Method

One of the simplest ways of addressing an objection is using what is called *The Feel, Felt, Found Method.*

If you've ever been in sales, then you've heard this one before. It's a method of overcoming objections that has definitely stood the test of time and is <u>very easy to learn</u>. Most people who've had any sales training at all learned this very early on in their career...and it works very well in Network Marketing.

There are three parts to it:

1. ***"I understand how you feel."*** It lets your prospect know that you <u>heard</u> what they had to say and you can personally relate to what they just said. You're empathizing with them.

2. **"Other people I've worked with have felt the same way."** You're essentially letting the person know that what they just said is fairly common and other people have had the same feeling or experience. It also provides them social proof that other people *like them* have had the same exact feelings.

3. **"What they found after doing this was that after having done 'A' was that 'B' happened."** In this case, 'A' is what you're looking for your prospect to do, and 'B' is the actual real and positive result of doing whatever it is you're looking for them to do.

This method can be used in virtually every situation where you get an objection from someone, either about your products or your business opportunity.

Let me give you a couple of examples.

Objection: "Your product seems expensive."

Response: *"I understand that you might feel there may be cheaper options out there. One of my best customers felt the same way you do. However, when he saw the results he got from taking our product and found that he didn't have to spend so much on eating out while at work, he realized that he was not only saving money, but feeling a lot better about his health."*

Objection: "I don't have the time."

Response: *"I understand how you feel. I have a lot of very busy people I work with that feel exactly like you do...*

very busy and not much free time. However, when they got involved in the business they quickly realized that they could build the business in their own time, whenever they felt like it and were able to create some really great results working the business with just a few hours a week."

You get the point. It will be good for you to look at all the different objections that might come up and practice this method until it becomes effortless for you. A little practice goes a long way in helping you address objections using this very simple and proven method.

The Neutralize, Confirm and Reposition Method

This one is pretty cool too and is also very easy to learn. My friend Michael Bernoff does this all the time and is a master at it.

Many times when someone gives you an objection, there is a deeper answer. In other words, while they voice a specific objection...the real reason may actually be different than what they are stating to you.

People oftentimes expect that you're going to argue with them. As I mentioned before, you never want to argue with a prospect giving you an objection. Instead, you can do it like this...

YOUR PROSPECT: *"I just don't have the money."*

They're stating that they don't have the money to get started.

YOU: *"Okay."*

You're <u>neutralizing</u> their objection by agreeing with them.

YOU: *"Well, is that the only thing that is preventing you from getting started?"*

You're <u>confirming</u> that their lack of funds is the real reason for them not starting in your business.

YOUR PROSPECT: *"Yes...I don't have any extra funds to start a business."*

YOU: *"What makes you feel that you don't have the money to start the business?"*

Now...you're asking them a <u>question to uncover</u> the real reason they may be giving you the objection.

YOUR PROSPECT: *"Well...I'm just not sure that I can actually make money at this."*

They've just given you their real objection. They aren't entirely sure they can do the business and don't want to part with the money unless they know it will work for them.

YOU: *"Wow...I guess I failed to show you that this isn't a business where we just toss you in and send you out to try and figure it out all on your own. When you enroll with* *me, I work personally <u>with you</u> to help you get into profit quickly, in addition to the fact that we have an entire training program with our company that teaches you step-by-step how to do this business."*

You've now <u>repositioned</u> the objection for them and provided some assurance that you'll be there to help them get into profit.

YOU: *"If you knew that there was a complete training program that teaches you step-by-step how to build this and you have me personally working with you to help you get into profit quickly, you'd want to do that, wouldn't you?"*

At that point, you'd want to go back to them and <u>re-ask</u> for their commitment to start the business.

Again...this one takes a little practice. I would suggest that you look at the different objections people give you and practice this strategy as well.

In fact...this would be a great training topic for you to cover with your personal team during any training events that you might be doing for your company.

Think about how powerful and professional your team will be when you train them on how to overcome objections using these two strategies!

How to Handle the 20 Most Common Objections

I'm going to cover the most frequent objections or questions you get in Network Marketing and give you some additional suggestions on how to address them.

Of course, you can use *The Feel, Felt, Found Method* or *The Neutralize, Confirm and Reposition Method* for any of these objections.

You'll see below that there are lots of different ways to address these common objections, in addition to the two methods I've already mentioned.

Objection #1: "I don't have the time."

We hear this all the time! In fact...it's probably the number one objection you get from people, or at least very close to it.

They may respond with *"I don't have the time."* Or, *"I'm just too busy."*

The thing you want to be thinking about is this...

Is time the real issue? Or, is there something deeper than that? Perhaps they aren't convinced the business works or it will work for them.

Here's how I might handle this situation, other than the two methods I've already described.

YOUR PROSPECT: *"I just don't have the time!"*

YOU: *"How does it make you feel to say that?"*

YOUR PROSPECT: *"I don't like it. I don't have the time for anything right now."*

YOU: *"Well...do you have a plan to change that situation?"*

YOUR PROSPECT: *"No...not really."*

YOU: *"Well...would you like to see one?"*

I may even ask them something like, *"What is taking up all of your time?"*

The more you know, again...without arguing or getting defensive, the better off you'll be. You're looking to help them SOLVE whatever problem it is that they may be facing.

What is the prospect's perception of how much time the business takes? They may think that they have to work the business full-time or that it takes a lot of hours to make their business work.

Even taking the time to ask them, *"How much time do you think this business takes to be successful?"* may be enough to alter their thinking.

I built my last business working only a handful of hours a week and got it to over 6-figures. They may be thinking that it takes a 40-hour week to do this. Obviously, the more time someone can commit, the faster they'll increase their income. But, for a lot of people...they do this very part-time.

Objection #2: "I don't have the money."

Not having the money is a key reason to do this business! Yet, we hear this objection very frequently in Network Marketing.

Here are a couple of different ways of handling the *"I don't have the money"* or *"I can't afford it"* objections.

Again...don't be afraid to ask the question, *"How does it make you feel to say that?"*

Be careful with your TONE of voice so you don't sound condescending when you ask it. But...if you're coming from a place of empathy, they may open up to you and tell you exactly how they feel. Most likely, it doesn't feel good and they'd like to change that situation. Nobody likes to say, *"I can't afford it."*

YOUR PROSPECT: *"I don't have the money."*

YOU: *"I get it. I've worked with a lot of people who felt they didn't have the money. Are you actively doing anything right now to help you change that situation in your life?"*

YOUR PROSPECT: *"No. I feel stuck. I'm working three jobs and barely making ends meet."*

YOU: *"Are you ready to do something about that so you never have to say 'I don't have the money' again?"*

Another way of finding out what the real reason is could be asking a direct question.

YOUR PROSPECT: *"I can't afford it."*

YOU: *"I hear what you are saying...but tell me this. Is it really that you don't have the money, or is that your polite way of telling me NO? It's okay if you're not interested. This business isn't for everybody."*

Sometimes it's okay to simply let someone go and uncover that they simply aren't interested in doing the business. I'd rather have a person be honest with me than try to make me feel good.

You can try this one as well:

YOUR PROSPECT: *"I can't afford it."*

YOU: *"I hear what you are saying and totally understand. If I could show you a plan to get all of your money back and get you into profit within your first 30 days, would you be more likely to join?"*

Sometimes people simply don't see the VALUE in the opportunity and aren't entirely convinced they can make money at it.

I've done this one several times:

YOUR PROSPECT: *"I don't have the money to get started."*

YOU: *"No problem. Let me ask you a hypothetical question. If your car broke down tomorrow, and you'd lose your job and not be able to get your kids to and from school...and it cost you $1,000 to get your car fixed, would you come up with the money to fix your car, even if it required you being extremely creative to make it happen?"*

YOUR PROSPECT: *"If that was the case, I'm sure I would."*

YOU: *"So...is what you're telling me then that you aren't entirely convinced that the value of this business isn't enough to justify the investment to get started?"*

YOUR PROSPECT: *"Yeah...I guess so."*

YOU: *"So...if I could show you a plan that you were convinced would help you get into profit very quickly, would you be more likely to be creative and make this business happen for you?"*

As I said, there are a lot of ways for you to help address these common objections. I use all of them...depending on how I feel in whatever situation I might find myself.

Objection #3: *"Is this a pyramid?"*

This is actually a fun one to handle. Most people who ask you, *"Is this a pyramid?"* or say something like, *"This sounds like a pyramid scheme"* don't even know the difference between a legitimate Network Marketing company and an illegal pyramid scheme.

Years ago, I used to get into an argumentative discussion over the differences of a pyramid and corporate America.

I'd even draw out a corporate structure for them, attempting to make my case. However, I found that it was simply a waste of time...and I soon learned that arguing or becoming defensive got me nowhere with that objection.

YOUR PROSPECT: *"Is this a pyramid?"*

YOU: *"Absolutely not. Why? Is that what you're looking for? I don't do pyramids. They're illegal. Do you have another question?"*

People will often stop dead in their tracks when you use that one!

You can very quickly move on to any of their other real concerns after you've addressed that one in the way I just referenced...or by using one of the other methods I've already given you.

Whatever you do, don't argue with them. They probably don't even know the difference, so you end up arguing with someone who doesn't even know what they are talking about.

Objection #4: "Is this a scam?"

No one wants to be scammed or be involved in a scam or scheme.

People want to participate in legitimate, real businesses, not fly-by-night, money games that don't last.

Network Marketing, as you already know...is a proven and very viable means of moving products and services to end users. The profession isn't on trial, and we shouldn't treat it as such.

Be easy on these people that give you this objection. They're simply telling you that they don't want to participate in something that isn't real.

YOUR PROSPECT: *"This sounds like a scam to me."*

YOU: *"What exactly makes it sound like scam to you? I certainly wouldn't want to be associated with something that's a scam."*

YOUR PROSPECT: *"Well...this whole thing about finding people to put money in. It all sounds suspicious to me."*

YOU: *"It isn't about getting people to put money in. If it was...I'd be suspicious too. Anyone who has ever started a business of their own had to invest both their time and, perhaps, a little money to get it started. Our focus is on moving products to end-users. If I could show you some information and allow you to do your own research on it so you knew that it's real, would you take the time to look*

*at it? No pressure from me...you can simply do your own
due-diligence and get back to me. Does that sound fair?"*

As with all of these questions and objections, there are
different ways to handle them. I want to make sure I arm
you so that you can handle them like a pro!

Objection #5: "I've tried Network Marketing before and it didn't work for me."

What you want to do with this type of objection is find
out the real story behind it.

YOUR PROSPECT: *"I tried one of those things before and
it didn't work out for me."*

YOU: *"Really? Tell me about that. What happened?"*

YOUR PROSPECT: *"Well...I signed up for something once
and I never had anyone help me. I lost money at it."*

YOU: *"Wow! I'm sorry to hear that. I'd be soured too.
If you knew for sure that you had someone to actually
support you and not abandon you after you signed up,
would you be willing to take a little leap of faith and
have a different, and more positive experience this
time around?"*

Find out exactly what their previous experience was in
Network Marketing. The more calm you are and the more
you dive in to find out what happened with them before,
the more likely you'll end up sponsoring them into
your business!

Objection #6: "I don't know how to start a business."

Many people who get into Network Marketing have never done a business before and are fearful and unsure as to what to do.

Giving them a little vote of confidence can go a long way in helping them ease their mind.

I'd suggest using *The Feel, Felt, Found Method* with this one.

YOUR PROSPECT: *"I don't know anything about starting a business."*

YOU: *"I totally understand how you feel. A lot of people who get into Network Marketing for the first time feel exactly the same way. In fact, I did too! What I found was that there was a lot of really great training for brand new people that teaches you exactly how to do the business. I was very concerned before I signed up until I started to plug into the training and support provided for free by the company, and it helped me to understand how to build it!"*

Helping someone feel comfortable in their decision is a big part of moving them closer to making the commitment to join you!

Objection #7: "I need to think about it."

This is a tricky one in which you'll need to dig deeper in order to find out what the REAL objection is, in most cases.

"I need to think about it" may mean they need to do just that...let it sink in. It may also be a stall or a polite way of them saying NO to you. Sometimes people are actually afraid to say NO and so instead, they avoid the whole idea altogether.

Sometimes I'm very direct and the conversation may go like this:

YOUR PROSPECT: *"I need to think about it."*

YOU: *"What specifically do you need to think about? Perhaps I can help clear things up or give you additional information so you can make a better decision for yourself?"*

There's nothing wrong with also asking them a direct statement like, *"What additional questions do you have?"*

They still may need to think about it...or let it sink in. I wouldn't apply too much pressure here. Your job is basically being a tour guide and helping them navigate through whatever information it is your company provides so your prospect gets everything they need to make the right decision for them.

This is also a great time to use your company's product guarantee or even business guarantee (if you have one), to incentivize them to take action now.

Most companies offer a money-back guarantee...almost certainly on their products, and many even on the business packages offered. It's pretty standard practice in consumer safety for companies to offer this option.

So...your conversation might go something along these lines:

YOUR PROSPECT: *"You know...I really need to think this over."*

YOU: *"I can totally appreciate that. It's a big decision and one that I didn't take lightly either. Mind if I offer you a suggestion?"*

YOUR PROSPECT: *"No...not at all."*

YOU: *"Our company offers a 100% money-back guarantee on all of our products and distributor packages. What I've done with a number of people is enroll them into the business and allow them to, more or less, feel out the business for their first 30 days. If, for whatever reason, you decide that you don't want to continue the business within your first month, the company will refund you 100% of your money....so you really have nothing to risk at all. Would that make sense to you?"*

Of course, be sure to check and see what exactly your company's guarantee is on either your products or your business before offering this alternative to them. But...it can often be enough to get a person to enroll right then and there.

Objection #8: "I'm not a sales person."

It may come out as *"I don't like sales"* or *"I don't like selling,"* or any variation of that.

A lot of people have an idea in their mind that selling is somehow pressuring an individual into doing something they don't really want to do. And...honestly, some very high-pressure sales people do that, which gives selling a bad name.

Good sales people see what they do as offering something of value in exchange for money...and the value of their offering is worth more than the money people are paying for it.

Others simply don't "see" themselves as salespeople... and want nothing to do with it.

Some good questions to ask to gain some clarity with your prospect are:

"Have you done sales before?"
"What is your past experience in selling?"
"What is it about selling that you don't like?"
"What selling do you believe is involved in Network Marketing?"

Of course, you don't have to ask all of those questions. Use whatever suits you in the situation you in which you find yourself.

A couple of variations on dealing with this are:

YOUR PROSPECT: *"I don't like sales."*

YOU: *"Well...you're going to love this then because we focus more on sharing information, rather than actually being sales people."*

Now...I personally have a <u>very strong</u> opinion about Network Marketing and Direct Sales. We DO sell. We don't just share stuff. Having sales and strong communication skills is an advantage to you. While it's not "traditional sales", we definitely sell our products and services to end-users.

So...be careful that you don't under-sell (pun intended) the fact that we aren't sales to someone. This is one of those debatable subjects amongst Network Marketers. Some see it is selling as I do...and many others look at it purely as sharing. I'd say the industry is a bit of both.

Here's another angle:

YOUR PROSPECT: *"I'm not good at sales."*

YOU: *"What makes you say that?"*

YOUR PROSPECT: *"I was in sales before and wasn't very good at it."*

YOU: *"Well...to be honest with you, this business may not be for you then, because we do a lot of talking to people and sharing information about our products and business. Do you like working with people?"*

I don't have a problem letting a prospect off the hook. If they feel they don't really like selling, they may not enjoy what we do.

As you can see...there's more than "one way to skin a cat" as they say. Not sure if that's even a nice phrase...but you get the point!

Objection #9: "I don't know anyone."

Sometimes people are concerned that they don't know very many people and think that you <u>have to</u> know lots of people to be successful in this business.

This objection may come in different forms like "I don't know enough people" or "I don't have anyone to talk to about this."

Either way...it's an easy one to address.

YOUR PROSPECT: *"I don't know anyone."*

YOU: *"What's great about this business is that it's not always about who <u>you</u> know, but who you'll meet. Do you like meeting and getting to know new people?"*

Or...you could go this route if you wanted to:

YOUR PROSPECT: *"I don't think I know enough people to build this right."*

YOU: *"That's not a problem at all. We can show you a bunch of different ways to find and meet new people to build this business. If you knew that there were ways to build this business, without knowing lots of people, would you want to do this?"*

What we always want to be doing in overcoming objections or addressing their questions is have flexibility. You have a lot of different directions to head in conversations.

You're not stuck...ever, and you always have options and different directions to go in your conversations with your prospects.

Objection #10: "I don't want to talk to my friends or family."

This one is fairly similar to them not knowing anyone. Most Network Marketing companies are primarily driven...at least in the early stages through warm market prospecting. Very seldom...and I mean very seldom, do you see a company where their primary means of driving new business is based on everyone doing cold market prospecting as their initial business building strategy.

This particular objection also comes in a few different forms, including questions like, *"Do I have to talk to my friends and family to do this?"*

Or...they may even say, although it is rare, *"I don't want to bug my friends and family."*

If someone presents me with this objection, here's how I may respond:

YOUR PROSPECT: *"I don't want to talk to my friends and family about this."*

YOU: *"Great...so if I told you that you could build this business without talking to your friends and family, are you ready to get started right now?"*

You see how easy that is? No arguing, no being on the defensive. Simple.

Objection #11: *"I'd like to try the products first."*

Even though many people see this as an objection, it's actually a buying sign. If someone tells you that they want to try your products first...that's <u>great</u>! Get them to try your products!

Some of your best distributors will come from first being happy, satisfied customers on your products.

No need to argue with that one!

YOUR PROSPECT: *"I'd like to try your products first."*

YOU: *"Great! Do you know which products you want to try or would you like for me to recommend some to you?"*

Now...this whole overcoming objection thing doesn't seem so hard anymore, does it?

Objection #12: "I need to talk with my wife/husband, etc."

When someone says this to you, it may actually be that they really want to share this information with their spouse because they don't make decisions without them. Lots of families work that way.

Sometimes it's another one of their ways of saying NO, without actually saying so.

The best response I've found in handling this type of objection is something like this:

YOUR PROSPECT: *"I need to talk with my wife about this first."*

YOU: *"Not a problem! Would your wife be working the business with you...or do you need to simply get her OK before you proceed?"*

YOUR PROSPECT: *"She may be working the business with me, but I definitely don't want to make a decision without her."*

YOU: *"OK. Why don't we do this? Instead of you running the information by her, why don't we set up a time for all of us to get together so she can see/hear the exact same thing that you did? That way she has the same information that you've just reviewed. It makes more sense to do it that way, doesn't it?"*

Objection #13: "I want to see how you do first."

The only time you will get this objection is with your warm market. Your friends will sometimes test you and play a little hard ball. All they really want to know is whether the business works or not.

They'll either say, *"I want to see how you do first"* or ask you how much money you are making.

If you've been in for a year and are not making very much money...or none at all, I can see how that would be a hard question to answer. I've been there...I was in that exact situation when I first started. In fact, I was two years into my first Network Marketing company and hardly making anything.

Here's a couple different ways to handle it:

YOUR PROSPECT: *"How much money are you making at this?"*

YOU: *"I'm glad you asked. I just got started myself and really haven't made much yet, but my business partner has been doing this for quite awhile and is doing very well with it. Why don't I introduce you two so you can hear her story on how it's worked for her?"*

If you've been in for a long while and maybe not treated the business very seriously until now, you may respond in a different way:

YOUR PROSPECT: *"How much money are you making?"*

YOU: *"You know what? I've been on their products for over a year and really focused on simply using them. And...because I got such great results in taking them, I decided to start building the business. So...I haven't really made much yet since I'm just getting started on the business end."*

If they pull the *"I want to see how you do first"* routine, this is what I would do.

YOUR PROSPECT: *"I want to see how you do in this first."*

YOU: *"That's fine. Just so you know, if you end up waiting and I do really well, you may end up missing out on having some people in your group that would be on your team if you had joined earlier. But...that's fine if you want to wait. I can get back to you at another time and keep you abreast of my progress."*

Overcoming objections isn't about you "winning" every single time someone throws up a roadblock in the process. Sometimes you can simply walk away and be ok with it.

Don't ever get emotionally attached to the outcomes when you are prospecting. If you set your mind on always recruiting someone and end up feeling disappointed when they don't join you, you're going to be in for a very long haul. Not everyone joins...and that's just fine.

Objection #14: "I don't want to be on auto-ship."

Not all companies have a compulsory auto-ship.

Many companies that are product focused offer auto-ship as a convenient way of delivering products to people so they don't run out.

If someone tells me that they don't want to be on auto-ship, my response would be along the lines of this: YOUR PROSPECT: *"I really don't want to be on auto-ship."*

YOU: *"Okay. If you didn't have to be on auto-ship, would you want to get started right now in building your business?"*

Objection #15: "It's too expensive."

I actually covered this one earlier when I was going through *The Feel, Felt, Found Method.*

However, this objection can come in different forms like *"I can get the product cheaper elsewhere."*

Other than using the method I described earlier for this particular objection, you could ask a few questions to dig a little further if you wanted to find out what the real issue is:

"Is price the most important thing for you?"

"Would you be willing to pay a little bit more if you

knew the quality was superior, kind of like paying for a Mercedes versus buying a Volkswagen?"

They may even give you the objection by asking, *"Why do I have to pay to get in?"*

This is obviously someone who doesn't understand that starting a business requires start-up capital. Very few businesses are ever free to start. Here's how I'd handle this objection:

YOUR PROSPECT: "Why do I have to pay to get in?"

YOU: *"That's a great question. You're starting your own business, not working for someone else. Any business that you're going to start on your own is going to require some money to get started. The great thing about our business model is that you can start for very little money...especially in comparison to starting a franchise, which could cost you $50,000 to over one million dollars.*

And...because you're now becoming a self-employed business person, you get all sorts of great tax advantages that you don't have as an employee. If you knew that additional deductions would be available, effectively putting more money in your pocket, simply by starting a business, would that be of interest to you?"

I just showed you something <u>HUGE</u> that most people never use in their prospecting efforts. There are a lot of tax advantages to owning and running your own business. Why not use that as a way of helping someone become more inclined to take action?

"If you knew that owning a business would potentially save you thousands of dollars and <u>keep</u> more of your hard earned money, you'd want to do that, wouldn't you?"

Objection #16: "I got burned before."

Anytime I hear this one, there has to be something behind it. Very seldom do people actually "get burned."

This objection may come in another form like *"My friend got burned in one of those things before."*

Obviously, in this case...you want to find out what their actual experience was in the program where they say they got burned.

I've done a <u>ridiculous amount</u> of prospecting in my career.

In other words, I've probably seen and experienced everything there is to see when it comes to responses from people.

Remember this; many times when people say they got burned, they simply never really did anything with the business and are assessing blame on the company, their sponsor, or anything else...<u>but</u> themselves.

People call me in my office all the time to tell me their sob story on how they are "failures" in Network Marketing...yet when I dig for real answers, it's not that they are failures at all, it's that they never really <u>did</u> anything!

Here's how you can pretty easily address this one and find the real answer:

YOUR PROSPECT: *"I got burned in one of those things before."*

YOU: *"Oh wow! I'm sorry to hear that. What do you mean exactly? What happened?"*

YOUR PROSPECT: *"Well...I signed up in a company and my sponsor never did anything to help me and left me stranded."*

Now you have what they feel is the REAL reason. Simply give them some assurance that you will be there for them and not "drop the ball" the way their previous sponsor did.

The truth may also be that they <u>did</u> get burned. Rarely have I ever met <u>anyone</u> who had a company take their money and run.

In fact...in the 25+ years I've done this, I cannot even actually recall anyone who had that happen to them. I've talked to people who joined a company and it <u>later</u> went out of business...but I wouldn't exactly call that being "burned."

Objection #17: "I don't like doing parties."

Lots of Network Marketing companies are driven by having their reps do in-home presentations, home parties or PBR's (Private Business Receptions) to present their business.

Some people simply <u>don't</u> want to host parties. Now... if you're in a Party Plan company or one that <u>is</u> driven primarily by doing in-home presentations, and you have a prospect that throws up this objection, you have to be truthful with them.

Sure...I could say, *"Hey....no worries man. You don't have to do parties."*

And...that may be the truth. They can do whatever they want. But...if they aren't willing to do what the entire <u>culture</u> of their company does as a primary means of building the business, they are going to be at a disadvantage.

Let's say you had a prospect say, *"I don't want to talk to people at all."*

You wouldn't come back and say, *"That's fine. You can build this business without talking to people."*

Why not? It would be a bold-faced lie. You cannot be a Network Marketer without talking to people. It's what we do!

IF you do parties or in-homes as your primary way of showing your business and you get this objection, here is one way to respond:

YOUR PROSPECT: *"I don't want to do any parties."*

YOU: *"What is it about doing parties that you don't like?"*

YOUR PROSPECT: *"I just don't want to do anything at my house. It's a dump, and I'm ashamed of it."*

YOU: *"No problem. If I could show you how to build this business and not have to host parties at your house, would you be more inclined to want to do this? I'm happy to host them at my place!"*

All your doing is giving them some peace of mind and providing a different option for them.

If your business is built <u>without</u> doing lots of meetings, this is very easy to address:

YOUR PROSPECT: *"I don't want to do any parties."*

YOU: *"That's great...because it's not how we do it."*

YOUR PROSPECT: *"Oh....great! How's it done then?"*

YOU: *"We have a number of online and offline marketing tools that do all of the presenting for us...so you can literally build this business from your home without ever hosting a meeting!"*

This entire "Overcoming Objections" thing isn't actually that hard or intimidating after all, is it?

Objection #18: *"There's too much competition."*

Although a more rare objection, it does happen. It may come out a bit differently like, *"Isn't it saturated already?"*

From my experience, no company in the history of mankind has ever reached total market saturation. Yes…there are a few companies that are widely known by name, but to say that they have reached a market saturation level isn't accurate.

YOUR PROSPECT: *"I think it's too late. The market is saturated already."*

YOU: *"I understand how you feel. I've had a few other people say the exact same thing. What they found after actually joining the business and doing it was that very few people they talked to had even <u>heard</u> about our company before."*

All we really want to do is <u>ease the mind</u> of our prospects so they feel good in making a decision.

Objection #19: "My friend tried one."

This is another one where there is typically some kind of story behind it. Ask them about their friend's experience.

YOUR PROSPECT: *"My friend tried one of those things and it didn't work for her."*

YOU: *"Do you know exactly what happened for her?"*

YOUR PROSPECT: *"Not exactly. I know she signed up for something and never made any money."*

YOU: *"Is it possible that she may really not have <u>worked</u> at the business, or stuck to it for very long?"*

Just find out by asking. They may not even know anything!

I interviewed a very successful Network Marketer who wouldn't even consider doing Network Marketing for years. She had an "idea" in her mind, and it was based on literally <u>nothing.</u> She never had anyone she knew try one, she'd never tried one...literally no experience at all.

She just thought in her mind, *"Network Marketing. Bad."*

Finally...a friend convinced her to go to a meeting. And...it was after asking her a bunch of times. She finally gave in and went to the meeting.

She told me in the interview that she was kicking herself in the butt for blowing it off for so long. She went on to build an organization in that company of over 300,000 representatives in 23 countries!

Objection #20: "I looked your company up on Google and read something bad about it."

In the Information Age, people have access to things they never had before. You can look up information on anything using a search engine like Google.

You could be with the best company on the planet and still find stuff on Google that doesn't look good. In fact... there are people that <u>specifically</u> post things on Google to simply drive traffic to their website with headlines that say, *"Company X is a Scam!"*

Here's how I deal with the person who searches the web and finds something negative about my company.

YOUR PROSPECT: *"I looked your company up on Google and read something that sounded bad. I'm not sure I want to do this now."*

YOU: *"Can you tell me exactly what you saw?"*

YOUR PROSPECT: *"It was some website that said your company is a scam."*

YOU: *"I don't know if you realize this or not, but literally <u>anyone</u> can put up a post or article and say what they want on the Internet. It's not exactly the most accurate place to conduct your due diligence about any company."*

YOUR PROSPECT: *"Well...it said some pretty negative things."*

YOU: *"I understand how you feel. I've had other people look our company up online and see the same thing. What they found, however, after doing a little more research on the source of that information was that it was simply an online marketer using our company's name to drive traffic to their own website. If I could show you that we are in fact a really good company...and that what you're reading on the Internet is in fact <u>not true</u>, would you want to take a deeper look at what we are doing?"*

It's a really good idea for you to Google your company's name and find out what's out there so you can be prepared for this before it happens. While a great place to find information about virtually anything, Google or any other search engine should never be the primary resource that someone uses to conduct due diligence on anything.

Power Phrases and Questions for Your Arsenal

As a little add on here, I want to suggest to you some other statements, phrases or types of questions that you can use to help uncover answers in your recruiting efforts.

All of these can be used in different circumstances to help you uncover answers and be able to navigate more successfully through the objection handling process.

"Tell me more about..."
Helps you to find out more information.

"What do you mean exactly..."
Gives you some clarity with what they just said.

"So, what you're saying is...."
Another way of gaining clarity by repeating back to them what they actually meant from their previous statement.

"What will be different in your life a year from now when you do this?"
Gets them thinking about how their life will look like if they take action in this business.

"How important is it for you to change that?"
Again, helps you to get them thinking about whether or not it is a priority for them to change their current situation.

"Is there someone else you might know who..."
This is an opening door to a referral.

"Which of the two looks better to you?"
A way of asking a question that proposes two
positive options.

"This sounds pretty cool, doesn't it?" Or, any question
that ends in *"Don't you? Aren't they? Isn't it?
Wouldn't you?"*

Tie-down questions are an effective way of geting small
agreements along the way.

When I make phone calls, especially to professionals, I
follow a very specific "template" when engaging people
in conversations about Network Marketing. It helps to
understand <u>why</u> my calls work so well.

It's called my ***7 Steps to Yes Template,*** and you can get
that one on my website as well if you'd like. It's also free
to download here: <u>toddfalcone.com/free-gift-6</u>.

CHAPTER EIGHT
HOW TO CLOSE LIKE A PRO

If you're going to be successful in Network Marketing, then you have to get good at closing.

Yeah...I get that someone reading this may still be thinking that Network Marketing isn't "sales" and that "closing" is a sales term, but let's just agree that you have to be able to ask for the business, enroll them on your products or services, or put them into your business.

And...for this book, we're calling it closing. ·

Four Tips to Better Closing Ratios

1. ***Be Totally Present Throughout the Entire Process.***
   This means that you listen to what your prospect is saying and that you pay very close attention to their responses and actions. You do not want to be multi-tasking by sending emails or doing FaceBook status updates when you are on the phone with someone. Wherever you are, be there! You can't afford to miss out on something important they told you in the process.

2. *Always be Professional.* That means doing what you say you are going to do. You show up on time for follow-up meetings. You get them what you said you were going to get them. In other words, you <u>do</u> what you say. Never drop the ball. Ever.

3. *Pay Attention to Buying Signs.* People who ask questions are showing interest. That's a good sign. If they ask you questions about how the business is built, that's a sign. Make sure you listen for things they say and do that show they are interested.

4. *Know Your Packages and Your Products Well.* You'll be a much better closer when you understand the different options that are available to get someone started in your company and what the <u>benefits</u> are to your new recruit. You need to know this.

Very Simple and Powerful Closing Techniques

The great thing about teaching closing in Network Marketing is that it doesn't have to be complicated! Let me make this really simple for you.

Here's typically what happens in a prospecting situation:

You meet someone and establish some rapport. Or, you have a conversation with someone you already know.

You invite them to take a look at your products or business.

You schedule a time and present your business to that person.

You take their temperature and see how interested, how "hot or cold" they are.

You either sign them up now, or you schedule a follow up call or meeting with them, because they need further information.

You get back to them <u>on time</u> for your follow up meeting to answer their questions and address any objections they might have.

You ultimately get to the point where they begin to run out of questions and are either showing lots of interest or not.

You transition into a close.

Here's how I transition into a close with a prospect. By now, this person is showing me through their actions and through their questions that they are highly interested in the business. It should be pretty obvious at this point in the process.

Here's how you do it.

YOU: *"Do you have any other questions at all?"*

YOUR PROSPECT: *"No...I think you've answered all of them."*

YOU: *"Great. Let me tell you about the different options you have in starting with us."*

In most cases, I don't actually ASK a closing question. I actually suggest that they start, and explain what options are available to them in doing so.

If I were to ask, my question would simply be, *"Are you ready to get started?"*

That question would always be followed by showing them the different options they have in getting started. So, I don't even ask the question most of the time. But, you can certainly do so if you'd like.

This may be the place where you get objections from your prospects. But now, since you know how to handle them, you're covered.

Let's go back to this closing scenario and I'm going to use a couple of fictional packages for this example.

YOU: *"Great. Let me tell you about the different options you have in starting with us.*

The first option is simply starting out with our distributor kit, which costs $49 to get started. This is more for a person who really isn't ready to take immediate action... someone who wants to try it out for a bit.

The other option, and what most business builders do, and what I did, was start with the Business Builders Package. It gives you extra tools, a website to build your business, full access to our back-office so you can track your business growth and enough product for you to gather your first few customers.

The Business Builders Package is $499 and is the best way for someone to start if they want to position themselves for success.

Which option makes the most sense to you?"

Let your prospect decide what is best for them. I suggest the different options and explain to them the <u>benefits</u> of joining at those optional levels. But...in the end, they need to decide for themselves.

Almost every Network Marketing company offers different start up options for people. It is <u>imperative</u> that <u>you understand what's in them, and the benefits they provide.</u>

Critical Note: People will almost <u>always</u> do what you do. That's why leading by example is so critical. If you started out with the $49 kit, it's going to be quite difficult for you to enroll someone at the $499 Business Builders Package. It's hard to sell something that you don't personally own.

They may even ask you, *"How did you get started?"*

You can't lie to them and say you started with the Business Builders Package when you started with the $49 kit. However, you can likely "upgrade" if your company provides that option.

That way if someone asks you that question, you can respond with:

"You know, when I first signed up, I just got the kit. But, I quickly realized that if I was going to be successful and treat this business as a <u>business</u>, I needed to have the Business Builders Package, so I upgraded to it."

Let's go back to my closing scenario again...

YOU: *The Business Builders Package is $499 and is the best way for someone to start if they want to position themselves for success. Which option makes the most sense to you?"*

YOUR PROSPECT: *"The Business Builders Package seems like the way to go."*

YOU: *"Let's get you started. Do you have a credit card handy?"*

YOUR PROSPECT: *"Let me get it. Hang on for a second."*

<u>I never</u>, ever send someone to my website to go sign up on their own. I always do the enrolling and enter their information from my computer.

You may have paper applications to fill out...and that's fine. If so, you'd probably be sitting <u>with</u> the person when that's happening.

Most Network Marketing companies allow you to simply go to your website, enter their information...and get them enrolled.

The reason I don't let them do it on their own is because it eliminates anything that would cause them to stop in the process. YOU control the situation. And...you maintain control of it.

I will then go to the place on my website where I enter their information, and do it. Now back to where we left off...

YOU: *"Let's get you started. Do you have a credit card handy?"*

YOUR PROSPECT: *"Let me get it. Hang on for a second. Okay, got it."*

Now...with your website open on the enrollment page, you take down their information and enter it.

"What's the proper spelling of your name?"
"Your billing address?"
"Shipping address?"
"Phone number? Email?"
"What do you want your username to be for your website?"
"How about a password?"
"What's your Social Security Number or Federal Tax ID Number?"

The information that needs to be entered to enroll someone is pretty standard from company to company.

Their name or business name (if they are signing up as a company) will be required, in addition to a physical address, phone number, e-mail address, Social Security Number or Federal Tax ID Number (if in the United States and signing up as a company), and credit card information. A username and password may also be needed to set-up a personal website.

If you live outside of the US, it may be some other Tax ID Number that is required. If you live outside of the US, you know what that is for your country.

There are two places that many people get hung up in the process...and something that you need to master and be comfortable with starting right now!

Those two "hang up" spots for people are:

- Asking for their Social Security Number or Tax ID Number.
- Asking for their credit card details.

You have developed enough trust with your prospect at this point where you shouldn't be worried about asking for this information.

And...because it is a requirement in the enrollment process, it's not a place where you want to get stuck or fearful.

Here's how to do it when you get to this stage:

YOU: *"What's your Social?"*

YOUR PROSPECT: *"555-55-5555."*

YOU: *"Visa, Mastercard, Discover or Amex?"*

YOUR PROSPECT: *"Visa."*

YOU: *"Great...go!"*

That little phrase is effective. *"Great! Go."* Your prospect knows that you are asking for them to give you their credit card number, which you will be entering into the website to process the payment.

YOU: *"Expiration date? CVV code on the back?"*

Then...you press the "Submit" button, or whatever your button says to process the payment and finish the enrollment process.

No need to plant a negative seed and say anything like, *"I need to get your credit card information. I hope you are okay with that?"*

We take credit cards every day in this business...and you need to get used to it.

If they ask, *"Why do you need my Social Security Number?"*

Simply respond with something like this:

"When the company issues you a check, they need to make sure they have your Social Security Number or Federal Tax ID Number for tax purposes in sending you

your 1099 Form at the end of the year. They can't pay you unless that information is entered into the system."

If they have a personal challenge with providing you that information and are concerned about their privacy, don't get defensive. Simply explain to them how it works. Back to the closing scenario...

YOU: *"Expiration date? CVV code on the back?"*

Once you have gotten all their information and come to the end of your sign up process, you press the button and process the order.

What will likely happen now is a screen will come up that shows you the new recruit's Independent Distributor Number for your company.

I'll tell them to simply grab a pen and paper to write down that number.

You've just enrolled a new distributor! Congratulations!!!

Now...it's time to help them get started in building their new business with you!

Be sure to take action with them immediately. Help them get going. Be a good sponsor...and make a commitment to work with your new recruits to create a success story. Don't just send them on their way in hopes that it will work out for them.

CHAPTER NINE

GETTING PEOPLE STARTED RIGHT

As we wrap up, I want to end with helping you to understand how to create more successes with the new people you are sponsoring into your business.

While you've just closed someone into enrolling...it isn't the <u>end</u> of the process, it's actually the beginning!

Six Strategies for Creating Success with Your New Reps

1. ***Get Them into Action Immediately.*** Once you've enrolled someone, the best thing you can do is help them gather their first few customers and distributors. This means taking action <u>now</u> and making some calls or doing some meetings with them. One thing you do <u>not</u> want to do is send them out on a two-week training mission to learn everything before they take action. Yes...training is very important, but taking action right now is the best thing you can do for them. They'll learn as they do it.

2. ***Introduce Them to the Team.*** As soon as I've enrolled a new distributor, one of the first things I like to do is have them meet other people on the team. I'll make calls with them to my upline leaders and welcome them aboard. It helps to cement that person's decision to join...and makes them realize that there are lots of other like-minded people involved in the business that have a vested interest in their success. They're also a lot more likely to reach out for help to other upline leaders if they've already gotten acquainted with them.

3. ***Help Them Set Up Their Systems or Tools.*** You'll want to make sure your new recruit has everything in order. Make sure they know your call or training schedule, when and where events take place, what tools they'll be using to present, or other resources they'll be using to help them build their business.

4. ***Assist Them in Creating Their Own Product Story.*** Whether you market a product or service, your new rep is most likely going to be personally using whatever it is you sell. Teaching them how to use your product or service is very important. Don't assume they'll know how to take them or use them. Show your new rep how to do it, and be sure to follow up with them regularly...especially during the first 30 days to make sure that using your product or service has become a habit.

5. ***Plug Them into Training.*** Make sure you point out exactly where your new distributor can access education and training to help them learn how to

do this business properly. Getting a new person to a live event within their first month can be extremely powerful. If you've attended any event for your Network Marketing company, you know how powerful this is in cementing a person's decision to engage. Events help a person establish belief and confirm they've made the right decision.

6. **Work Where You're Deserved, Not Where You're Needed.** I heard that phrase the first week I started in Network Marketing over 25 years ago. You'll have people enroll that engage and take action...and others who do nothing. You want to be investing your time with people who deserve your time and attention based on the actions they take. If a person says they want to be successful, yet does nothing...their actions are showing you that they aren't exactly ready. If you've done a great job of helping a new rep get started and haven't abandoned them, then you've done your part. They have to choose to engage. If they don't, then make sure you invest your valuable time in working with people who not only "say" they want to succeed, but "show you" through their actions.

There are two primary activities that we do in Network Marketing...prospecting and team building. You first have to know how to effectively prospect, recruit and gather customers for the products or services you market.

Then...once you've enrolled a new person in your business, you have to be good at sponsoring them, which is far beyond simply getting them signed up into your business.

Once you've begun to work with a new recruit, you start focusing some of your time on helping others on the team building side of the business. This is where you are working *with* them to help them achieve success.

I have a really great tool to help you on the team building side of the business that you can download off of my site. It's called my ***Explosive Growth Cheat Sheet.***

You can get it right here: ToddFalcone.com/free-gift-5.

Conclusion

Well my friend, it's been fun! Before we part ways, I have some very important words for you in getting the most from this book.

How Reading This Book Becomes a Profitable Experience for You

Don't ever confuse information with application. People read books all the time and do nothing with them.

It is never the *acquisition* of information or knowledge that makes the difference in someone's life. It's good to have, but it's what you <u>do</u> with it that makes all the difference in the world. Action is, quite literally...everything!

There's a phrase I say on almost every stage I speak at throughout the world. I want you to remember the phrase and live it.

Soak and Apply.

Average people read and do nothing with the knowledge given to them. It's why they remain average. Successful people, on the other hand, gather knowledge with the specific intent of putting that information into action to create a specific result.

Soak in the strategies. Apply them. Put them into action in your business today until you master them. Then, pass your knowledge and skills forward.

Life is better when you're FEARLESS!

Todd Falcone

About the Author

Todd Falcone is one of the leading independent trainers in the Network Marketing industry. Having been in the profession for over 25 years, he brings a wealth of knowledge from real and personal experience in building as a Network Marketing distributor.

Now as a retired distributor, Todd <u>exclusively</u> teaches so that others may experience the benefits and opportunities provided to those who choose to dedicate themselves to the profession.

For the past 15 years, Todd has been a coach, trainer and advisor to some of the most successful men and women in the entire Network Marketing profession.

He speaks to audiences all over the world, and is regularly featured as a keynote speaker at Network Marketing conferences and trainings.

Todd Falcone Resources

Plug into Todd's training newsletter and blog by going to: ToddFalcone.com.

You can order any of Todd's bestselling audio programs at ToddFalcone.com, including:

Cracking the Code to Success in Network Marketing
Everything you ever wanted to know about building and sustaining a successful Network Marketing business.

Insider Secrets to Recruiting Professionals
Learn exactly how to recruit professional, high quality people into your business.

Little Black Book of Scripts
This script book literally puts the words in your mouth for every possible situation you'll find yourself in as a Network Marketer.